Design: Jill Coote
Recipe Photography: Peter Barry
Jacket and Illustration Artwork: Jane Winton,
courtesy of Bernard Thornton Artists, London
Editors: Jillian Stewart, Kate Cranshaw and Laura Potts

CLB 3517
Published by Grange Books,
an imprint of Grange Books PLC,
The Grange, Grange Yard, London.
© 1994 CLB Publishing,
Godalming, Surrey, England.
All rights reserved.
Printed and bound in Singapore
Published 1994
ISBN 1-85627-434-9

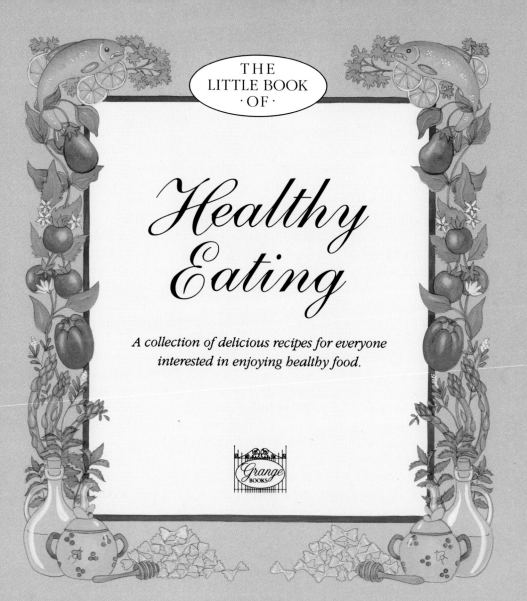

THE
LITTLE BOOK
·OF·

Healthy Eating

A collection of delicious recipes for everyone
interested in enjoying healthy food.

Grange
BOOKS

Introduction

Magazines and newspapers regularly publish articles expounding the latest theories about what foods we should or should not eat and why, so there can certainly be said to be no lack of information on what is believed to constitute a healthy diet. Yet, sadly, much of the advice with which we are bombarded is contradictory, leaving many puzzled as to what they should be eating.

Variety is at the heart of a pattern of healthy eating. As no one type of food contains all the proteins, fats, carbohydrates, vitamins and minerals needed by the body, it is vital to eat a wide variety of food stuffs to ensure that the balance needed to keep the body healthy is maintained.

Protein is essential for the well-being of the body, promoting the growth and repair of tissues and among other things helping to make the antibodies which enable the body to fight infection. Meat, fish and dairy products are all good sources of protein, and ones with which most people are familiar. Grains, pulses and nuts, however, also contain some proteins (though they are not complete proteins and must be eaten in the correct combinations in order for the body to get maximum benefit). Modern diets tend to rely too heavily on animal proteins and neglect vegetable proteins, which contain no cholesterol or saturated fat. A healthy diet should use vegetable proteins to make up a larger proportion of the body's protein requirement and reduce the intake of fat-rich, animal proteins.

It is therefore particularly important to try to reduce the amount of red meat included in your diet, as it contains high levels of saturated fat and cholesterol. Cholesterol, a fat-like substance, is transported around the body in the bloodstream and although small amounts are necessary for the correct functioning of the body, a high level in the blood stream may lead to cholesterol deposits in the blood vessels. A build-up of such fatty deposits thickens the walls of the vessels, making it harder for the heart to pump blood around the body and so putting it under strain. Although no conclusive link between dietary cholesterol and levels of cholesterol in the blood has yet been made, it is wise to eat meats which are known to be low in cholesterol, such as chicken, as well as eating more meat-free meals. Fish is another great addition to a healthy diet, particularly fatty fish such as mackerel, which contains oils which are believed to be cholesterol reducing.

Fresh fruit and vegetables play an important role in a well-balanced diet as both are a good source of fibre and are rich in the vitamins and minerals needed for the body to function properly.

A good, well-balanced diet is the key to a long and healthy life and, as the wide range of delicious recipes in this book show, food that is healthy need never be tasteless or lacking in imagination. Including a selection of starters, meat and fish dishes, as well as desserts, this book provides the perfect introduction to the delights of healthy eating.

Gazpacho

SERVES 4

Gazpacho is a typically Spanish soup which is served well chilled, accompanied by a selection of fresh vegetables.

PREPARATION: 20 mins plus chilling

460g/1lb ripe tomatoes
1 onion, chopped
1 green pepper, diced
½ cucumber, chopped
2 tbsps stale white breadcrumbs
2 cloves garlic, crushed
2 tbsps red wine vinegar
570ml/1 pint tomato juice
Salt and freshly ground black pepper

Accompaniments
½ cucumber, diced
10 spring onions, chopped
225g/8oz tomatoes, skinned, seeded and
    chopped
1 large green pepper, diced

1. Cut a small cross in the top of each of the tomatoes, and plunge into a bowl of boiling water for a few seconds.

2. Carefully peel the skin away from the blanched tomatoes. Discard the skin and roughly chop the tomatoes, removing the tough cores.

Step 2
Carefully peel the skin away from the blanched tomatoes using a sharp knife.

3. Put the roughly chopped tomatoes into a liquidiser or food processor, along with the onion, pepper and cucumber. Blend until finely chopped.

4. Put the chopped vegetables into a bowl with the breadcrumbs, garlic, vinegar and tomato juice. Mix well to blend evenly and allow to stand for 15 minutes.

5. Season the soup thoroughly, then push through a fine meshed sieve using the back of a wooden spoon and working well to press all the vegetables through, but keeping the pips out of the resulting purée.

6. Chill the soup well before serving, surrounded by bowls containing the accompaniments.

Mediterranean Aubergines

SERVES 2-4

These delicious stuffed aubergines can be served as an accompaniment to a main meal for four or as a lunch dish for two.

PREPARATION: 25 mins
COOKING: 40 mins

2 small aubergines
30g/1oz polyunsaturated margarine
1 small onion, finely chopped
1 clove garlic, crushed
120g/4oz tomatoes, skinned
150g/5oz long grain rice, cooked
2 tsps fresh chopped marjoram
Pinch cinnamon
Salt and freshly ground black pepper

1. Wrap the aubergines in foil and bake in an oven preheated to 180°C/350°F/Gas Mark 4, for 20 minutes or until softened. Allow to cool.

2. Cut the aubergines in half, lengthwise, then using a serrated teaspoon or grapefruit knife, carefully scoop out the pulp leaving a 1.25cm/½-inch border to form a shell.

3. Melt the margarine in a frying pan and gently sauté the onion and garlic until they are just soft.

4. Chop the aubergine pulp roughly and stir into the pan along with the onions. Cover and cook for about 5 minutes.

Step 2
Carefully scoop the pulp out of each aubergine half with a serrated spoon or grapefruit knife.

5. Quarter the tomatoes and remove and discard the pips. Chop the tomato flesh roughly and stir into the cooked aubergine and onion mixture, along with the cooked rice, marjoram and cinnamon. Season with salt and pepper.

6. Carefully pile the rice filling into the aubergine shells and arrange them in an ovenproof dish or on a baking tray. Cover with foil.

7. Return to the oven and bake for 20 minutes. Serve hot, garnished with a little finely chopped parsley if wished.

Tomato and Pepper Ice

SERVES 4-6

Similar to frozen gazpacho, this starter is ideal for serving on warm summer days.

PREPARATION: 15 mins plus 2 hrs freezing

6 ice cubes
120ml/4 fl oz canned tomato juice
Juice of 1 lemon
1 tsp Worcestershire sauce
½ small green pepper, very finely chopped
½ small red pepper, very finely chopped

1. Put the ice into a thick plastic bag and break into small pieces using a rolling pin or small hammer.

2. Put the broken ice into a blender or food processor, along with the tomato juice, lemon juice and Worcestershire sauce. Blend the mixture until it becomes slushy.

Step 2 Blend the ice, tomato juice, lemon juice and Worcestershire sauce until it becomes a smooth slush.

Step 5 During the freezing time, keep stirring the tomato and pepper ice with a fork, to prevent the mixture from becoming a solid block.

3. Pour the tomato mixture into ice trays and freeze for ½ hour, or until it is just half frozen.

4. Remove the tomato ice from the freezer trays and put it into a bowl. Mash the tomato ice with the back of a fork until the crystals are well broken up.

5. Mix in the chopped peppers and return the tomato ice to the freezer trays. Re-freeze for a further 1½ hours, stirring occasionally to prevent the mixture from solidifying completely.

6. To serve, allow the tomato ice to defrost for about 5 minutes, then mash with the back of a fork to roughly break up the ice crystals. Serve in small chilled glass dishes or in tomato shells.

Courgette, Caper and Anchovy Salad

SERVES 4

The secret of this salad is to slice the raw courgettes really thinly.

PREPARATION: 15-20 mins

460g/1lb courgettes
1 small onion, thinly sliced
1 tbsp capers
4-6 canned anchovy fillets, chopped
1 tbsp anchovy oil (drained from the can of
    anchovy fillets)
2 tbsps olive oil
2 tbsps tarragon vinegar
Juice of ½ lemon
Salt and freshly ground black pepper to taste

1. Top and tail the courgettes, and slice them very thinly with a sharp knife, food processor or mandolin.

2. Mix the sliced courgettes with the onion, capers and chopped anchovy fillets.

3. Mix the anchovy oil, olive oil, tarragon vinegar and lemon juice together; add salt and pepper to taste.

4. Stir the dressing into the prepared salad ingredients.

Salade Paysanne

SERVES 6

This salad can be made with any selection of fresh vegetables, so whether its winter or summer, there's no excuse for not serving a delicious fresh salad.

PREPARATION: 20 mins

4 spring onions
½ cucumber
3 carrots
6 large tomatoes, skinned
10 button mushrooms
3 stems celery
1 green pepper, chopped
15-20 tiny cauliflower florets
15-20 radishes, quartered
1 tbsp chopped watercress, or mustard and cress
2 sprigs fresh coriander, or parsley, chopped
8 lettuce leaves for garnish

Dressing
½ tsp salt
½ tsp freshly ground black pepper
2 tbsps cider vinegar
1 tbsp lemon juice
60ml/4 tbsps olive or vegetable oil
Pinch mustard powder
Liquid sweetener to taste

1. Trim the spring onions and slice them diagonally into thin slices.

2. Peel the cucumber and quarter it lengthways. Use a sharp knife to remove the

Step 6 Whisk all the dressing ingredients together using a fork or balloon whisk, until the mixture becomes thick and cloudy.

soft, seedy centre, discard this, and dice the remaining flesh.

3. Peel the carrots and slice them thinly, cutting the carrots diagonally with a sharp knife.

4. Quarter the skinned tomatoes and cut away the tough green cores.

5. Thinly slice the mushrooms and celery. Cut the pepper in half lengthways, discard the seeds and pith then chop the flesh.

6. Mix together all the dressing ingredients. Whisk thoroughly using a fork, or balloon whisk, until the mixture becomes thick and cloudy.

7. Arrange the lettuce leaves on a serving dish. Mix all the prepared vegetables together, and pile on top.

8. Just before serving, spoon a little of the dressing over the salad and serve the remainder separately in a small jug.

Vegetable and Olive Casserole

SERVES 6

The addition of vinegar and capers gives this refreshing vegetable dish a sharp twist to its flavour.

PREPARATION: 30 mins plus standing time
COOKING: 25 mins

1 aubergine
Salt
140ml/¼ pint olive, or vegetable oil
1 onion, thinly sliced
2 red peppers, chopped
2 sticks celery, thickly sliced
460g/1lb canned plum tomatoes, chopped and
    sieved
2 tbsps red wine vinegar
1 tbsp sugar
1 clove garlic, crushed
Salt and freshly ground black pepper
12 pitted black olives, quartered
1 tbsp capers

1. Cut the aubergine in half lengthways and score the cut surface deeply, in a lattice fashion, with the point of a sharp knife.

Step 1 Score the cut surface of the aubergines in a lattice pattern, using the point of a sharp knife.

Step 6 Simmer the casserole, uncovered, over a low heat until the juice has thickened and reduced.

2. Sprinkle the cut surface liberally with salt, and leave to stand for 30 minutes. Rinse thoroughly under running water, then pat dry and cut it into 2.5cm/1-inch cubes.

3. Heat the oil in a large frying pan and add the onion, peppers and celery. Cook gently for about 5 minutes, stirring occasionally until the vegetables have softened but not browned.

4. Add the aubergine to the pan and mix well to coat thoroughly with the oil. Continue cooking gently for 5 minutes.

5. Add the sieved tomatoes to the pan, along with the remaining ingredients, except for the olives and capers. Cover and simmer for 5 minutes.

6. Add the olives and capers and continue cooking gently, uncovered, for 15 minutes, or until most of the liquid has evaporated and the sauce has thickened and reduced.

Seviche

SERVES 4

*In this traditional Mexican dish the raw fish is 'cooked' in a mixture
of oil and lime juice.*

PREPARATION: 20 mins plus 24 hrs standing time

460g/1lb fresh cod fillet, skinned
Juice and grated rind of 2 limes
1 small shallot, finely chopped
1 green chilli, seeded and finely chopped
1 tsp ground coriander
1 small green pepper, sliced
1 small red pepper, sliced
4 spring onions, finely chopped
1 tbsp chopped parsley
1 tbsp chopped coriander
2 tbsps olive oil
Freshly ground black pepper
1 small lettuce, to serve

1. Using a sharp knife cut the fish into very thin strips across the grain. Put the strips into a large bowl and pour over the lime juice.

Step 1 Cut the cod fillet across the grain into very thin slices.

Step 3 After refrigerating for 24 hours, the fish should have a cooked appearance.

2. Stir in the grated lime rind, shallot, chilli and ground coriander. Mix well.

3. Cover the bowl with cling film and refrigerate for 24 hours, stirring occasionally during this time to ensure that the fish remains well coated in the lime.

4. Mix the sliced peppers, spring onions and the fresh herbs together in a large bowl.

5. Put the fish mixture into a colander and drain off the juice. Add to the pepper mixture and stir in the oil, mixing well to coat evenly. Add freshly ground pepper to taste.

6. Finely shred the lettuce and arrange on a serving plate. Spread the fish mixture attractively over the lettuce and serve immediately, garnished with slices of lime, if wished.

Aubergine Bake

SERVES 6

Aubergines are wonderfully filling vegetables with very few calories – the ideal ingredient in a calorie controlled diet.

PREPARATION: 30 mins
COOKING: 40 mins

---

2 large or 3 medium-sized aubergines
2 tsps salt
140ml/¼ pint malt vinegar
2 tbsps vegetable oil
2 large onions, sliced into rings
2 green chillies, seeded and finely chopped
425g/15oz can chopped tomatoes
½ tsp chilli powder
1 tsp crushed garlic
½ tsp ground turmeric
8 tomatoes, sliced
280ml/½ pint natural low fat unset yogurt
1 tsp freshly ground black pepper
90g/3oz Cheddar cheese, finely grated

---

1. Cut the aubergines into 5mm/¼-inch thick slices. Arrange the slices in a shallow dish and sprinkle with 1 tsp of the salt. Pour over the vinegar, cover and marinate for 30 minutes.

2. Drain the aubergine well, discarding the marinade liquid. Press the slices into a colander using the back of your hand, to remove all the excess vinegar.

3. Heat the oil in a frying pan and gently sauté the onion rings until they are golden brown.

4. Add the chillies, the remaining salt,

Step 7 Spoon half the tomato sauce over the aubergine slices in the gratin dish.

chopped tomatoes, chilli powder, garlic and turmeric. Mix well and simmer for 5-7 minutes until thick and well blended.

5. Remove the sauce from the heat and cool slightly. Blend to a smooth purée in a liquidiser or food processor.

6. Arrange half of the aubergine slices in the base of a lightly greased shallow ovenproof dish.

7. Spoon half of the tomato sauce over the aubergine, cover with the remaining aubergine, and then top with the rest of the tomato sauce and sliced tomatoes.

8. Mix together the yogurt, black pepper and cheese, and pour over the tomato slices.

9. Cook the bake in an oven preheated to 190°C/375°F/Gas Mark 5, for 20-30 minutes, or until the topping bubbles and turns golden brown. Serve hot straight from the oven.

Chicken with 'Burnt' Peppers and Coriander

SERVES 4

'Burning' peppers is a technique for removing the skins which also imparts a delicious flavour to this popular vegetable.

PREPARATION: 30 mins
COOKING: 1½ hrs

2 red peppers, halved and seeded
1 green pepper, halved and seeded
60ml/4 tbsps vegetable oil, for brushing
1 tbsp olive oil
2 tsps paprika
¼ tsp ground cumin
Pinch cayenne pepper
2 cloves garlic, crushed
460g/1lb canned tomatoes, drained and
   chopped
3 tbsps fresh chopped coriander
3 tbsps fresh chopped parsley
Salt, for seasoning
4 large chicken breasts, boned
1 large onion, sliced
60g/2oz flaked almonds

1. Put the peppers, cut side down, on a flat surface and gently press them flat. Brush the skin side with 2 tbsps of the vegetable oil and cook them under a hot grill until the skin chars and splits.

2. Wrap the peppers in a clean tea-towel for 10 minutes to cool then carefully peel off the charred skin. Chop the pepper flesh into thin strips.

3. Heat the olive oil in a frying pan and gently fry all the spices and garlic for 2 minutes, stirring to prevent the garlic from browning.

4. Stir in the tomatoes, herbs and seasoning. Simmer for 15-20 minutes, or until thick. Set aside.

5. Heat the remaining vegetable oil in a flameproof casserole, and sauté the chicken breasts, turning them frequently until golden on both sides.

6. Remove the chicken and set aside. Gently sauté the onion in the oil for about 5 minutes, or until softened.

7. Return the chicken to the casserole with the onion and pour on about 280ml/½ pint of water. Bring to the boil. Cover the casserole and simmer for about 30 minutes, turning the chicken occasionally to prevent it from burning.

8. Remove the chicken from the casserole and boil the remaining liquid rapidly to reduce to about 90ml/3 fl oz of stock. Add the peppers and the tomato sauce, stirring well.

9. Return the chicken to the casserole, cover and simmer very gently for a further 30 minutes, or until tender.

10. Arrange the chicken on a serving dish with a little of the sauce spooned over. Sprinkle with the flaked almonds and serve any remaining sauce separately.

Herrings with Apples

SERVES 4

The addition of apples beautifully complements the delicious and wholesome flavour of herring.

PREPARATION: 15-20 mins
COOKING: 50 mins

---

4 herrings, cleaned
2 large dessert apples
4 large potatoes, peeled and sliced
1 large onion, thinly sliced
Salt and freshly ground black pepper
140ml/¼ pint dry cider
60g/2oz dried breadcrumbs
60g/2oz polyunsaturated margarine
1 tbsp fresh chopped parsley

---

1. Cut the heads and tails from the herrings and split them open from the underside.

2. Put the herrings, belly side down, on a flat surface and carefully press along the back of each fish with the palm of your hand, pushing the backbone down towards the surface.

3. Turn the herrings over and with a sharp knife, carefully prise away the backbone, pulling out any loose bones as well. Do not cut the fish into separate fillets. Wash and dry them well.

4. Peel, quarter, core and slice one of the apples. Lightly grease a shallow baking dish and layer the potatoes, apple and onions, seasoning well with salt and pepper between layers.

Step 3
Carefully lift the backbone away from the fish with a sharp knife, pulling any loose bones out at the same time.

5. Pour the cider over the top potato layer and cover the dish with foil. Bake in a preheated oven at 180°C/350°F/Gas Mark 4, for 40 minutes.

6. Remove the dish from the oven and arrange the herring fillets on the top. Sprinkle the breadcrumbs over and dot with half of the margarine.

7. Increase the oven temperature to 200°C/400°F/Gas Mark 6 and return the dish to the oven for about 10-15 minutes, or until the herrings are cooked and brown.

8. Core the remaining apple and slice into rounds, leaving the peel on. Melt the remaining margarine in a frying pan and gently sauté the apple slices.

9. Remove the herrings from the oven and garnish with the sautéed apple slices and chopped parsley. Serve at once.

Veal with Sorrel Stuffing

SERVES 6

Fresh sorrel has a delightful flavour, if it is not available use fresh spinach instead.

PREPARATION: 25 mins
COOKING: 1 hr

900g/2lbs rolled joint of veal
120g/4oz low fat soft cheese with garlic and
    herbs
120g/4oz sorrel, finely chopped
2 tsps fresh oregano or marjoram, chopped
60g/2oz walnuts, finely chopped
Freshly ground black pepper
60g/2oz plain flour
½ tsp paprika
1 egg, beaten
120g/4oz dried breadcrumbs
45g/1½oz polyunsaturated margarine, melted

---

1. Unroll the veal joint and trim off some of the fat from the outside using a sharp knife.

2. Put the cheese, sorrel, oregano or marjoram, walnuts and black pepper into a bowl. Mix

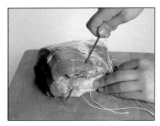

Step 2 Sew the ends of the joint together using a trussing needle and strong thread.

Step 2 Spread the filling ingredients evenly over the inside of the joint of meat.

together using a round bladed knife or your hands, until the ingredients are well bound together. Spread this filling over the inside of the veal. Roll the veal joint up, swiss-roll fashion, and sew the ends together with a trussing needle and thick thread.

3. Dredge the veal roll with the flour and sprinkle with the paprika. Press this coating well onto the meat using your hands.

4. Brush the floured joint liberally with beaten egg and roll it into the dried breadcrumbs, pressing gently to make sure that all surfaces are thoroughly coated.

5. Place the coated veal on a baking sheet, brush with the melted margarine and roast in a preheated oven at 160°C/325°F/Gas Mark 5, for 1 hour, or until the meat is well cooked.

6. Allow to stand for 10 minutes before slicing and serving hot, or chill and serve cold.

Tarragon Grilled Red Mullet

SERVES 4

Red mullet is a very decorative little fish that is now readily available at fishmongers and supermarkets.

PREPARATION: 10 mins plus marinating
COOKING: 10-16 mins

4 large or 8 small red mullet, gutted, scaled,
    washed and dried
4 or 8 sprigs of fresh tarragon
60ml/4 tbsps vegetable oil
2 tbsps tarragon vinegar
Salt and freshly ground black pepper

1. Rub the inside of each mullet with a teaspoonful of salt, scrubbing hard to remove any discoloured membranes inside. Rinse thoroughly.

2. Place a sprig of fresh tarragon inside each fish.

Step 1 Rub the insides of each fish with a teaspoonful of salt, scrubbing briskly to remove any discoloured membranes.

Step 3 Using a sharp knife, cut 2 diagonal slits on the side of each fish, taking great care not to cut right through the flesh.

3. Using a sharp knife cut 2 diagonal slits on both sides of each fish.

4. Mix together the vegetable oil, tarragon vinegar and a little salt and pepper in a small bowl.

5. Arrange the fish on a shallow dish and pour over the tarragon vinegar marinade, brushing some of the mixture into the cuts on the side of the fish. Refrigerate for 30 minutes.

6. Arrange the fish on a grill pan and cook under a preheated hot grill for 5-8 minutes per side, depending on the size of the fish. Baste frequently with the marinade while cooking, then serve with some sprigs of fresh tarragon, if liked.

Chicken with Lemon Julienne

SERVES 4-6

Lean chicken served with a tangy julienne of fresh vegetables makes a delicious main course.

PREPARATION: 40 mins
COOKING: 55 mins

---

1 × 1.4kg/3lb chicken
2 tbsps olive oil
30g/1oz polyunsaturated margarine
2 sticks celery
2 carrots
1 small onion, thinly sliced
1 tbsp chopped fresh basil
1 bay leaf
Juice and grated rind of 2 small lemons
140ml/¼ pint water
Salt and freshly ground black pepper
Lemon slices, for garnish

---

1. Cut the chicken into 8 pieces with a sharp knife or a cook's cleaver, cutting the chicken lengthways down the breastbone and through the backbone to halve it completely.

2. Cut the chicken in half again, slitting between the leg joint diagonally up and around the breast joint. Finally cut the drumsticks from the leg thigh joint, and the wings from the breast joints. Remove the skin from the chicken by pulling and cutting away with a sharp knife.

3. Heat the oil and margarine, in a large frying pan. Gently sauté the chicken pieces, turning them frequently to brown evenly. Remove and set aside.

4. Using a sharp knife, cut the celery and carrots into pieces 3.5cm/1½-inches long. Cut these pieces lengthways into long thin matchsticks.

5. Stir the carrots and celery into the chicken juices, along with the onion. Cook over a gentle heat for about 3 minutes or until just beginning to soften but not brown.

6. Stir in the basil, bay leaf, lemon juice and rind, the water, and salt and pepper. Mix well and cook for 2-3 minutes. Add the chicken and bring to the boil.

7. Cover the pan and reduce the heat. Allow the casserole to simmer for about 35-45 minutes, or until the chicken is tender and the juices run clear when the meat is pierced with a sharp knife.

8. Remove the chicken and vegetables to a serving dish and discard the bay leaf.

9. Heat the sauce quickly to thicken if necessary. Spoon the sauce over the chicken and garnish with the lemon slices.

Salmon Trout with Spinach

SERVES 6-8

PREPARATION: 35-40 mins
COOKING: 40 mins

1.1kg/2½lb fresh whole salmon trout, cleaned
900g/2lbs spinach, stalks removed
1 small onion, finely chopped
60g/2oz polyunsaturated margarine
60g/2oz walnuts, roughly chopped
120g/4oz fresh white breadcrumbs
1 tbsp fresh chopped parsley
1 tbsp fresh chopped thyme
¼ tsp grated nutmeg
Salt and freshly ground black pepper
Juice of 2 lemons
Watercress sprigs and lemon slices, to garnish

1. Carefully cut the underside of the fish to the tip of the tail. Sit it, belly side down, spreading the cut underside out to balance it.

2. Using the palm of your hand press down along the backbone, pushing the spine downwards. Turn the fish over and using a sharp knife, carefully pull the backbone away, cutting it out with scissors at the base of the head and tail.

3. Pull out any loose bones with a pair of tweezers then set the fish in the centre of a large square of lightly oiled foil.

4. Put the washed spinach into a large saucepan and sprinkle with salt. Do not add any extra water. Cover and cook over a moderate heat for about 3 minutes.

5. Turn into a colander and drain well, pressing with a spoon to remove all the excess moisture. Chop very finely using a sharp knife.

6. Fry the onion gently in 15g/½oz of the margarine until soft. Stir into the spinach along with the walnuts, breadcrumbs, herbs, nutmeg, salt, pepper and half the lemon juice. Mix well.

7. Push the stuffing firmly into the cavity of the fish, re-shaping it as you do so. Seal the foil over the fish, but do not wrap too tightly. Place in a roasting tin and bake in a preheated oven at 180°C/350°F/Gas Mark 4, for 35 minutes.

8. Carefully unwrap the fish and transfer to a large serving dish. Using a sharp knife, peel away the exposed skin of the fish.

9. Dot with the remaining margarine, sprinkle with the remaining lemon juice, and garnish.

Orange and Apricot Mousse

SERVES 4-6

This delicious light mousse makes an ideal end to any meal.

PREPARATION: 30-50 mins plus chilling time

2 oranges
3 × 400g/14oz cans apricots in natural juice,
    drained
Artificial sweetener to taste (optional)
25g/¾oz powdered gelatine
140ml/¼ pint natural low fat yogurt
2 egg whites
Extra orange rind, to decorate

1. Grate the rind from half of one orange using a fine grater, then cut all the oranges in half and squeeze out their juice.

2. Put the drained apricots, all but 3 tbsps of the orange juice, and the orange rind into a liquidiser or food processor, and purée until

Step 5 Allow the fruit purée and gelatine to chill in a refrigerator until it is just beginning to set.

Step 6 Fold the egg whites carefully, but thoroughly, into the thickening fruit mixture, taking care not to over mix.

smooth adding artificial sweetener to taste, if wished. Pour into a large bowl and set aside.

3. Sprinkle the gelatine over the orange juice in a bowl, and allow to stand until hydrated.

4. Set the gelatine mixture over a pan of hot water and leave to dissolve and clear.

5. Stir the gelatine mixture into the apricot purée, along with the yogurt, mixing well to blend evenly. Refrigerate for about 30 minutes until beginning to set.

6. Whisk the egg whites until they form soft peaks. Fold the whisked egg whites lightly, but thoroughly, into the partially set apricot mixture using a metal tablespoon.

7. Divide the fruit mousse evenly into serving glasses and chill until completely set.

Apple and Sultana Sorbet

SERVES 4-6

Sorbets make an ideal dessert for anyone on a low fat diet. Try this unusual combination for a real change of flavours.

PREPARATION: 10 mins, plus 4 hrs soaking and 6 hrs freezing.

850ml/1½ pints apple juice
60g/2oz caster sugar
45g/1½oz packet of dried apple flakes
120g/4oz sultanas
Few drops green food colouring, optional
1 egg white

---

1. Put 570ml/1 pint of the apple juice into a heavy-based saucepan along with the sugar. Heat gently, stirring until the sugar has dissolved. Bring to the boil and boil quickly for 5 minutes, then remove from the heat and leave to cool completely.

2. Put the apple flakes into a bowl along with the sultanas and remaining apple juice. Add enough of the syrup to cover the mixture, then

Step 3 Beat the apple and sultana mixture with a fork until it becomes a thick purée.

Step 7 Fold the whisked egg white carefully into the slushy ice before freezing completely.

allow to soak for 4 hours.

3. Mix the apple flake mixture together to form a pulp, adding the green colouring at this stage, if required.

4. Whisk the apple pulp into the remaining syrup, mixing thoroughly to blend evenly. Pour the apple mixture into a shallow container and freeze for 2 hours or until just beginning to set.

5. Break up the partially frozen ice using a fork or electric whisk, then return to the freezer tray and continue to freeze for another hour.

6. Break up the ice crystals again, but this time mash thoroughly until they form a thick slush.

7. Whisk the egg white until it is stiff, then quickly fold into the ice slush. Return to the freezer tray and freeze until completely solid.

8. Allow the ice to soften for 15 minutes before spooning into individual glass dishes.

Cherry Compôte

SERVES 6

Black cherries and apple juice combine perfectly in this tasty dessert.

PREPARATION: 20 mins
COOKING: 5 mins

680g/1½lbs fresh black cherries
420ml/¾ pint apple or grape juice
1½ tsps finely grated lemon rind
2 tbsps cornflour or arrowroot
3 tbsps brandy (optional)

---

1. Remove the stones from the cherries, using a cherry pitter or the rounded end of a potato peeler.

2. Put the pitted cherries into a saucepan, along with the apple or grape juice and the lemon rind. Bring to the boil over a moderate

Step 1 Remove the stones from the cherries using a cherry pitter or the rounded end of a potato peeler.

Step 4 Blend cornflour or arrowroot with 75ml/5 tbsps of the cherry juice.

heat, then simmer for 10 minutes, or until the cherries are gently poached.

3. Remove the cherries from the juice with a slotted spoon, leaving the juice in the saucepan. Arrange the cherries in a serving bowl.

4. Blend the cornflour with 75ml/5 tbsps of the cherry juice.

5. Add the blended cornflour or arrowroot to the cherry juice in the pan, and bring to the boil stirring constantly until the sauce has thickened. Stir in the brandy if using.

6. Pour the thickened cherry sauce over the cherries in the bowl, and chill well before serving.

Spiced Oranges with Honey and Mint

SERVES 4

An unusual combination of flavours blend to create this light and very refreshing dessert.

PREPARATION: 20 mins
COOKING: 5 mins

280ml/½ pint clear honey
420ml/¾ pint water
2 large sprigs of fresh mint
12 whole cloves
4 large oranges
4 small sprigs of mint, to garnish

1. Put the honey and the water into a heavy-based saucepan. Add the mint and cloves, and slowly bring to the boil.

2. Stir the mixture to dissolve the honey and boil rapidly for 5 minutes, or until the liquid is very syrupy.

3. Cool the mixture completely, then strain the syrup through a nylon sieve into a jug or bowl to remove the sprigs of mint and cloves.

Step 3 Strain the cool syrup through a nylon sieve into a jug or bowl to remove the sprigs of mint and cloves.

Step 4 Carefully pare the rind from one of the oranges using a potato peeler.

4. Using a potato peeler, carefully pare the rind very thinly from one orange, making sure that no white pith comes away with the rind. Cut the pared orange rind into very fine shreds with a sharp knife.

5. Put the shreds of orange peel into a small bowl and cover with boiling water. Allow to stand until cold, then drain completely and stir the strips into the honey syrup and chill well.

6. Peel the oranges completely, cutting off all the skin and especially the white pith.

7. Slice the oranges into thin rounds using a sharp knife. Arrange the orange rounds on four individual serving plates.

8. Pour the chilled syrup over the oranges and garnish with the small sprigs of mint just before serving.

Index